My Dream Journal

A book for recording the beautiful, bizarre & brilliant world of my dreams.

Journal Easy

© 2014

Name: Date:

Feeling:

Name: Date:

Feeling:

Name: Date:

Feeling:

Name: Date:

Feeling:

Name: Date:

Feeling:

Name: Date:

Feeling:

Name: Date:

Feeling:

Name: Date:

Feeling:

Name: Date:

Feeling:

Name: Date:

Feeling:

Name: Date:

Feeling:

Name: Date:

Feeling:

Name: Date:

Feeling:

Name: Date:

Feeling:

Name: Date:

Feeling:

Name: Date:

Feeling:

Name: Date:

Feeling:

Name: Date:

Feeling:

Name: Date:

Feeling:

Name: Date:

Feeling:

Name: Date:

Feeling:

Name: Date:

Feeling:

Name: Date:

Feeling:

Name: Date:

Feeling:

Name: Date:

Feeling:

Name: Date:

Feeling:

Name: Date:

Feeling:

Name: Date:

Feeling:

Name: Date:

Feeling:

Name: Date:

Feeling:

Name: Date:

Feeling:

Name: Date:

Feeling:

Name: Date:

Feeling:

Name: Date:

Feeling:

Name: Date:

Feeling:

Name: Date:

Feeling:

Name: Date:

Feeling:

Name: Date:

Feeling:

Name: Date:

Feeling:

Name: Date:

Feeling:

Name: Date:

Feeling:

Name: Date:

Feeling:

Name: Date:

Feeling:

Name: Date:

Feeling:

Name: Date:

Feeling:

Name: Date:

Feeling:

Name: Date:

Feeling:

Name: Date:

Feeling:

Name: Date:

Feeling:

Name: Date:

Feeling:

Name: Date:

Feeling:

Name: Date:

Feeling:

Name: Date:

Feeling:

Name: Date:

Feeling:

Name: Date:

Feeling:

Name: Date:

Feeling:

Name: Date:

Feeling:

Name: Date:

Feeling:

Name: Date:

Feeling:

Name: Date:

Feeling:

Name: Date:

Feeling:

Name: Date:

Feeling:

Name: Date:

Feeling:

Name: Date:

Feeling:

Name: Date:

Feeling:

Name: Date:

Feeling:

Name: Date:

Feeling:

Name: Date:

Feeling:

Name: Date:

Feeling:

Name: Date:

Feeling:

Name: Date:

Feeling:

Name: Date:

Feeling:

Name: Date:

Feeling:

Name: Date:

Feeling:

Name: Date:

Feeling:

Name: Date:

Feeling:

Name: Date:

Feeling:

Name: Date:

Feeling:

Name: Date:

Feeling:

Name: Date:

Feeling:

Name: Date:

Feeling:

Name: Date:

Feeling:

Name: Date:

Feeling:

Name: Date:

Feeling:

Name: Date:

Feeling:

Name: Date:

Feeling:

Name: Date:

Feeling:

Name: Date:

Feeling:

Name: Date:

Feeling:

Name: Date:

Feeling:

Name: Date:

Feeling:

Name: Date:

Feeling:

Name: Date:

Feeling:

Name: Date:

Feeling:

Name: Date:

Feeling:

Name: Date:

Feeling:

Name: Date:

Feeling:

Name: Date:

Feeling:

Name: Date:

Feeling:

Name: Date:

Feeling:

Name: Date:

Feeling:

Name: Date:

Feeling:

Name: Date:

Feeling:

Name: Date:

Feeling:

Name: Date:

Feeling:

Name: Date:

Feeling:

Name: Date:

Feeling:

Name: Date:

Feeling:

Name: Date:

Feeling:

Name: Date:

Feeling:

Name: Date:

Feeling:

Name: Date:

Feeling:

Name: Date:

Feeling:

Name: Date:

Feeling:

Name: Date:

Feeling:

Name: Date:

Feeling:

Name: Date:

Feeling:

Name: Date:

Feeling:

Name: Date:

Feeling:

Name: Date:

Feeling:

Name: Date:

Feeling:

Name: Date:

Feeling:

Name: Date:

Feeling:

Name: Date:

Feeling:

Name: Date:

Feeling:

Name: Date:

Feeling:

Name: Date:

Feeling:

Name: Date:

Feeling:

Name: Date:

Feeling:

Name: Date:

Feeling:

Name: Date:

Feeling:

Name: Date:

Feeling:

Name: Date:

Feeling:

Name: Date:

Feeling:

Name: Date:

Feeling:

Name: Date:

Feeling:

Name: Date:

Feeling:

Name: Date:

Feeling:

Name: Date:

Feeling:

Name: Date:

Feeling:

Name: Date:

Feeling:

Name: Date:

Feeling:

Name: Date:

Feeling:

Name: Date:

Feeling:

Name: Date:

Feeling:

Name: Date:

Feeling:

Name: Date:

Feeling:

Name: Date:

Feeling:

Name: Date:

Feeling:

Name: Date:

Feeling:

Name: Date:

Feeling:

Name: Date:

Feeling:

Name: Date:

Feeling:

Name: Date:

Feeling:

Name: Date:

Feeling:

Name: Date:

Feeling:

Name: Date:

Feeling:

Name: Date:

Feeling:

Name: Date:

Feeling:

Name: Date:

Feeling:

Dream Books, Films & Resources

Dream Books, Films & Resources

Dream Books, Films & Resources

Dream Books, Films & Resources